Questions Galore
Party Game Book

Grossest EWW EDITION

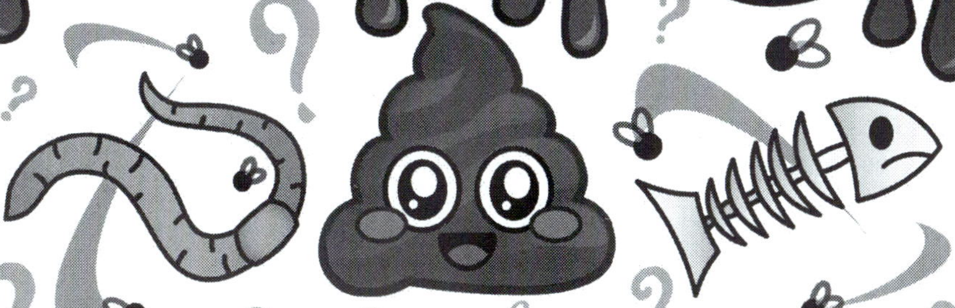

Sadie Word

Published in 2019 by Sadie Word
Copyright Illustrations © 2019 by Nyx Spectrum
All rights reserved. No part of this publication may be reproduced or transmitted in any form or by any means, electronic, or mechanical, including photocopy, recording or any information storage system and retrieval system without permission in writing by Publisher Sadie Word.
Printed in the United States of America

GREETINGS QUESTION SEEKERS!

Have you ever wanted to ride on the back of an Iguanodon dinosaur?

OR

Perhaps, you have been searching for a way to ask thought provoking questions to other humans for sport?

Well, this book can't help you with the Iguanodon until they come back from extinction, but it can help you start an engaging chat with other lifeforms!

This book is meant to inspire meaningful conversations with friends and family through oodles of thought provoking questions. Inspire loads of friendly inquiry with over 400 questions, enigmas, and conundrums!

So without any further ado, let the games begin!

DIRECTIONS:

Choose a reader.

Make sure to read the phrase, "Would you Rather-" at the beginning of each question.

The reader will read the first question and everyone will choose one of the choices given out loud.

Picking both or neither is not an option!

For the people who picked the least popular choice, ask them why they chose that?

You can also write the answers down on mini whiteboards, or make it into a points game!

PRO TIP:
Honestly, you really don't need to follow these directions. They have been included for those who like to follow the rules and need some boundaries. For all rule breaking rebels, please disregard these the direction pages and let pandemonium ensue!

Have your cellphone make farting noises for notifications
OR
Have your cellphone ringtone be Siri burping the ABC's?

Chug a whole glass of llama spit
OR
Eat an ice cream cone full of rainbow Unicorn Poop?

Always have onion breath
OR
Have garlic-scented B.O.?

Every song you now hear is made entirely of armpit sounds
OR
Have to squirt your drink out of your eye every time you take a sip?

Eat a five-course meal in a doctor's office filled with patients with the flu
OR
Swim a mile in a sewer?

Have ears the size of elephant ears
OR
Have a neck as long as a giraffe?

Have to wear cheetah print cowboy boots the rest of your life
OR
Wear neon green scuba diving flippers with gold rhinestones for the rest of your life?

Only be able to wash your clothes once a year?
OR
Only be able to bathe once a year?

Have someone snoop through everything in your room
OR
Have someone snoop through all your digital files and web searches?

Drink all your beverages like a dog
OR
Eat all your food whole like a snake?

Have your bed is infested with Bed Bugs
OR
Have you bed infested with Cockroaches?

Live with someone who burps very loudly every fifteen minutes
OR
Always follow someone closely up a long staircase while they constantly fart in your face?

Have a terrible sunburn all over your body and not be able to do anything but lie on your bed for a week
OR
Have really annoying hangnails on all of your toes and fingers constantly for a month?

Try to enjoy your meals that are always covered in a swarm of flies
OR
Sleep in the same room as someone that snores so loud it shakes the room?

Have a tongue like a Frog
OR
Have a nose like an Anteater?

Have a giant pimple on the tip of your nose
OR
Have a wart on the center of your chin?

Be woken up at dawn by the next-door neighbor's loud rooster
OR
Be woken up at 2 am by a screaming train behind your house?

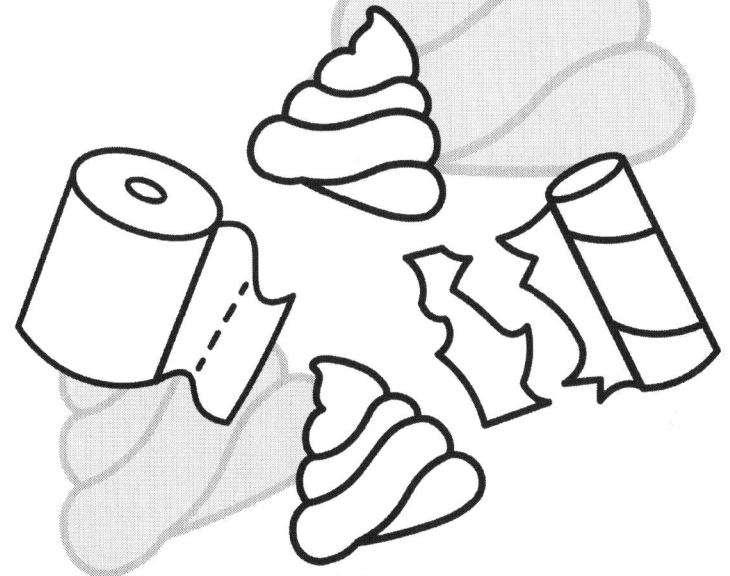

Never be able to eat any candy ever again
OR
Never be able to eat any baked desserts ever again?

Clean a toilet by scrubbing it
with a toothbrush
OR
Mow the lawn with nothing but
a pair of scissors?

Participating in a food fight
of fried bugs
OR
Jumping into a bathtub full
of cottage cheese?

Eat a meal that is totally burnt
to a crisp
OR
Drink a carton of chunky milk?

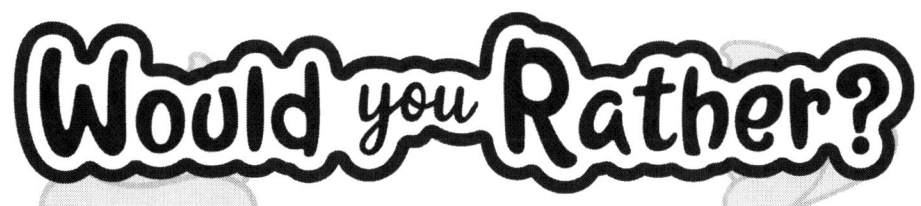

End up doing homework every waking moment you are not in class
OR
Do chores around the house every waking moment you are not in school?

Clean out fifteen dirty litter boxes every day
OR
Clean public restrooms at a gas station every day?

Drizzle Maple Syrup on all
your dinners
OR
Sprinkle Parmesan Cheese on
all your desserts?

Walk around in public with green
beans hanging out of your nose
OR
Walk around in public while wearing
your underwear over your pants?

Lick the bottom of your feet clean after walking everywhere barefoot all day
OR
Wash your hands with your own spit for a week?

Live on a small island made entirely out of dried bird poop for a month
OR
Live in your room for a week with 30 rats as your new roommates?

Bathe in ice-cold water for a month
OR
Bathe in murky lake water, where unknown creatures constantly brush your legs?

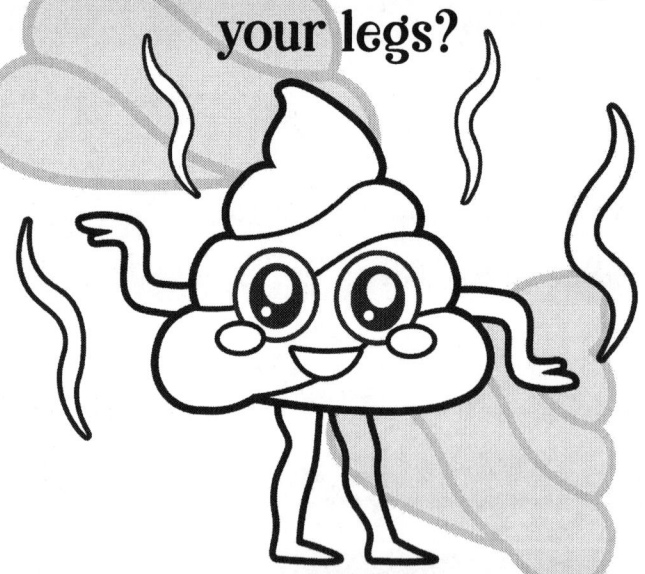

Get stuck on a roller coaster in the highest loop for 3 hours
OR
Get stuck in traffic with nothing to do or look at for 8 hours?

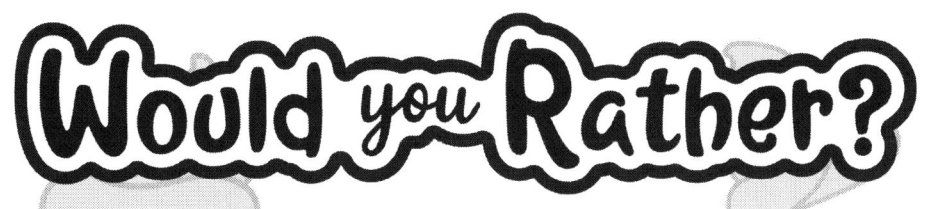

Have an airline always lose your luggage
OR
Always have to sit next to the smelly bathroom on a plane?

Have popcorn kernels that are stuck in-between all of your teeth for a year
OR
Have never-ending hiccups that annoy you and everyone around you for an entire year?

Clean hair out of the shower drain
OR
Wash a sink full of dishes with moldy food?

Wash your hair once a year
OR
Brush your teeth once a year?

Take up the hobby of braiding armpit hair
OR
Live your life with toenails that are two feet long?

Never be able to connect to wifi in your bedroom
OR
Only be able to connect to wifi in your bedroom and nowhere else?

Have the worst song stuck in your head every waking moment of the day
OR
Have your clothes get caught on every knob or handle you walk past?

Try to watch a movie that is interrupted by constant buffering every minute
OR
Try to watch all videos online with commercials that pop up every ten seconds?

Be bombarded every time you have a giant mouthful of food and someone asks you a question that needs a long wordy answer
OR
Any time you text someone a really important question it always takes them 72 hours to get back to you?

Not being able to grab that one strand of hair stuck to your tongue
OR
Always feeling like you need to sneeze, but never do?

Wear a sweater made out of cat hairballs
OR
Wear a sweater made out of shower drain hair?

Have a fly you can't catch constantly buzz around your head
OR
Have a tiny bug fly up your nose and you can't get it out?

Get sneezed on by everyone you walk past
OR
Get stranded on the toilet because someone forgot to replace the roll?

Forced to write a 50 page essay with your non-dominant hand
OR
Replace your hands with scissor hands?

Get hit by lightning
OR
Get spit on by a herd of llamas?

Have to sniff a baboon butt
OR
Wear a snake like a scarf for the day?

Eating a cup of straight Mayonnaise
OR
Eating a cup of straight Horseradish?

Everything you hear is now a fart noise
OR
Everything you smell is now a fart smell?

You constantly have styrofoam bits clinging to you
OR
Have every smoke detector in the house is out of batteries and are constantly beeping?

Everywhere you look there are animals pooping
OR
All the food you eat feels like Cottage Cheese in your mouth?

Mix a little of everything you have in the fridge together and drink the entire glass
OR
Have a Candle with every scent in the world and have it burning in your house all the time?

Would you Rather?

Get pooped on by a whole flock of pigeons
OR
Have an entire truckload of pig manure dumped over your head?

Be followed around all day by someone who burps really loudly in your face
OR
Be surrounded by people cracking their knuckles all day?

Have helium-filled poop
OR
Fart clouds of rainbow glitter?

Find old, used gum under your desk with your hand

OR

Watching someone eat that old, used gum and enjoying it?

Get covered in slime from head to toe

OR

Get covered in compost from head to toe?

Sweat so much your clothes are always drenched

OR

Always have your underwear full of little hermit crabs?

Eat a block of 50-year-old moldy cheese
OR
Eat all of your meals blended into slop, out of a pig's trough?

Only be able to drink prune juice
OR
Only be able to eat artichokes?

Live in a world where it rained anchovies twice a month
OR
Live in a world that hailed giant spitballs once a week?

Eat cotton candy made of belly button lint
OR
Always be wearing scary clown makeup?

Have your nose relocated to one of your big toes
OR
Have your ears relocated to your butt cheeks?

Have wings attached to your arms like bats
OR
Have a stinging tail like a scorpion?

Directions:

Don't Get Me Started is a funny twist on the Try Not to Laugh Challenge.

The group will choose one of the following topics for the first person to perform a rant.

The person destined to rant may do one of two things. They can either have an angry, heated rant about the topic. Or they can have an excited, and hysterical rant about the subject like it's the only thing they've ever loved!
Trust me, both are a hoot.

The ranting person must keep up their performance until they have everyone in the room laughing.

Take turns until everyone has done at least one rant!

People picking their nose in public

Decorating with Taxidermy animals

Piles of nail clippings

People who grow their nails
12 inches long

Squishing a slug with your barefoot

Popping a zit

The smell of low tide

Other people not flushing the toilet

Bird Poop

Dead Cockroaches

The smell of Wet Dog

Vinegar

DON'T get me STARTED!

Pig Manure

Hard-Boiled Eggs

Clogged Drains

Cracking knuckles

Burping

Cats coughing up Hairballs

Fried Bugs as Food

Sulfur

Smelling Skunk

Spitballs

The smell of cow manure

Chewing your hair

DON'T GET ME STARTED!

Sniffling

Really loud snoring

Smell of Gas

Eating live bugs

37

DON'T GET me STARTED!

Chewed gum stuck under things

People peeing on streets

Spitballs

Picking Wedgies

DON'T GET ME STARTED!

Spiders

Greasy Hair

Morning Breath

Dirty Socks

DON'T GET ME STARTED!

Maggots

Earwax in the shower

Stinky Cheese

Dog Breath

DON'T GET ME STARTED!

Cilantro

Walking through a Swamp

The word "Moist"

Garbage at the Dump

People who don't use Deodorant

DON'T GET ME STARTED!

Moldy Vegetables

Stepping in dog poop

Rotten Eggs

Super Slow Internet

DON'T GET ME STARTED!

Vomit

Perfume Isle

Ants all over your food

Bellybutton Lint

DON'T GET me STARTED!

Cannibals

Sewage

Screaming Babies in Public Places

Being sleep-deprived

DON'T GET ME STARTED!

Stubbing your pinky toe

Compost Piles

Tangled wires

Chunky Milk

DON'T GET me STARTED!

Spiders crawling all over you

Walking on legos

Dandruff

Porta Potties

DON'T GET ME STARTED!

Eye Gunk

Wet socks

People who have an annoying laugh

DON'T GET me STARTED!

Finding bugs in your food

Bee stings

Fungi

Smoke

DON'T GET ME STARTED!

Bad tasting Medicine

Quicksand

Bloody nose

Getting a shot at the doctors

Splinters you can't remove

DON'T GET me STARTED!

Yankee Candle Store

Itchy Mosquito bites

Tar Pits

Dirty Diapers

DON'T GET ME STARTED!

People with Runny Noses

Animals Pooping

Bad Fashion Sense

Which is WORSE?

Food Crimes Edition!

Believe it or not, but these foods have plagued the world at one time or another. It is up to you to decide which is the absolute worst food crime!

Directions:

The person with the next birthday coming up gets to be the reader.

Make sure to read the phrase, "Which is worse-" at the beginning of each question.

Have the reader ask a question and let everyone answer aloud.

You must pick the option that you would absolutely do not ever want to eat, not now, not then, nor ever again.

Give a point to the people who have the least popular choice. The first person to get to 10 points wins!

Which is WORSE?

Celery flavored Jello
OR
Turkey Gravy-flavored Soda?

Beef Jerky flavored Floss
OR
Yellow Curry-flavored Toothpaste?

Cheeseburger flavored Oreo
OR
Ramen-flavored Ice Cream?

Which is WORSE?

Liver Loaf
OR
Ribs in a Can?

Dip Cookies in Salsa
OR
Cover Spaghetti with Nacho Cheese?

Soy Sauce drizzled on Popcorn
OR
Drink a Latte out of an Avocado?

Which is WORSE?

Italian Sausage flavored Donut
OR
Salted Caramel Chicken Wings?

Gummy Bear Stuffed Burger
OR
Doritos Casserole?

Chicken Feet
OR
Sheep Brains?

Which is WORSE?

Lima Beans
OR
Kale Granola?

Chocolate Chip Cookie Grilled Cheese
OR
Lobster Mac and Cheese?

Garlic flavored Ice Cream
OR
Hawaiian Spaghetti Pizza?

Which is WORSE?

Tuna Eye Balls
OR
Fried Silk Worms?

Snow Cone made with Yellow Snow
OR
Spam straight out of the can?

Wasp Crackers
OR
Escargot (Snails)?

Which is WORSE?

Pickled Eggs
OR
Frog Legs?

Tofu Cookies
OR
TV Dinners?

Pickled Pork Rinds
OR
Pickled Pork Lips?

Which is WORSE?

Turnips
OR
Rutabaga?

Hospital Food
OR
Airline Food?

Turtle Soup
OR
Kangaroo Burger?

Which is WORSE?

Shark Fin Soup
OR
A Cup of Pickle Juice?

Orange juice in your Cereal
OR
Peanut Butter on Scrambled Eggs?

Dip French Fries in Milkshakes
OR
Hot Sauce on Fruit?

Which is WORSE?

Pickled Pig's Feet
OR
Vanilla Ice Cream with Soy Sauce?

Melted Chocolate on Ramen
OR
Hot Dog in a Peanut-butter and Jelly Sandwich?

Jellied Moose Nose
OR
Hotdog with a Twinkie Bun?

Which is WORSE?

Bacon Dog Treats
OR
Fish Cat Treats?

Soybeans
OR
Boiled Cabbage?

Peanut Butter Cup Stuffed Burger
OR
Cricket Milkshake?

Which is WORSE?

Black Licorice
OR
Blue Cheese?

Quail Eggs
OR
Anchovies?

Olives
OR
Raw Oysters?

Which is WORSE?

Slurp an Earthworm like Spaghetti
OR
Lick a Dung Beetle?

Spinach Baby Food
OR
Bologna Cake?

Tuna and Pear Pizza
OR
Prune-Stuffed Roast Pork?

Which is WORSE?

Creamed Possum
OR
Canned Scorpions?

Cottage Cheese
OR
Chocolate Cheese?

Mayo on Rice
OR
Dip a Bologna Sandwich in Coffee?

Which is WORSE?

Ketchup on Funfetti Cake
OR
Eat a raw onion like an Apple?

Spicy Salmon in a Waffle Cone
OR
Green Eggs and Ham?

Peeps Flavored Milk
OR
Ham and Bananas Hollandaise?

Which is WORSE?

Fruitcake
OR
Candy Corn?

Wasabi Peas
OR
Green Olives?

Tomato Soup Cake
OR
Hard-Boiled Eggs in Jello?

Which is WORSE?

Smoked Trout
OR
Sushi with Raw Fish?

Plain Greek Yogurt
OR
Grapefruit?

Broccoli
OR
Asparagus?

Which is WORSE?

Milk Chicken
OR
Tuna and Jello Pie?

Dark Chocolate
OR
Black Coffee?

Mushrooms
OR
Shrimp?

Which is WORSE?

Wet Dog Food
OR
Dry Cat Food?

Okra
OR
Raw Garlic?

Steak Pudding
OR
Lime Cheese Salad?

Which is WORSE?

Chicken Liver
OR
Turkey Gizzards?

Bacon Breath Mint
OR
Meatball flavored Bubblegum?

Silky Tofu
OR
Stewed Oxtail?

THANK YOU!

You are the most marvelous person for purchasing this book, thank you!

Congratulations on adopting this charming little edition into your home library! If it has brought you even a thimble full of joy, please consider leaving a review for it on Amazon.com

I shall wait patiently for your comments, my dear readers. Any guidance you are willing to bestow unto me helps me take another step closer to becoming the Grand Poobah of Game Books.

Help the cause, start a trend, and write a review!

—Sadie Word

Also by Sadie Word:

Also by Nyx Spectrum:

Manufactured by Amazon.ca
Bolton, ON